Bread Machine Cookbook

Easy and Delicious Bread Machine Recipes for No-Fuss
Baking at Home

Jennifer Tate

TABLE OF CONTENTS

INTRODUCTION

This book is a gift for all the **bread-lovers,** as each of its recipes has been tailored to comply with every existing bread baking rule and can be freely added to your daily-menu. Take a try on various crunchy loaves and choose your favorites. There is nothing like a bunch of fresh, fragrant bread with a piece of fancied butter, cheese or bacon for a great breakfast! All the kinds and flavors you could have only dreamt about are now there for you to cook and eat.

This book contains **bread machine recipes** divided into categories to make it easy for you. The recipes also have nutritional information to guide you on the amount of nutrients that you take into your body.

Start reading, and you will get into the world of **bread machine baking**. This book contains amazingly delicious **bread maker recipes** that are both easy to make and good for you.

Thanks for downloading this book. Enjoy reading and eating!

BASIC INGREDIENTS FOR BREAD BAKING

Flour, yeast, water, and salt work together to form the bread.

The combination of these common elements is the basis of our bread, but it is necessary to know these basic ingredients thoroughly to achieve a good result.

Let's start with the flour. It is an entire world but, to simplify things a little, we will say that it is nothing more than the result of the grinding of a cereal, seed or tuber. The most common flours for baking are wheat flour (there are many varieties of this cereal); oats; corn; rye; barley and even nuts like chestnut. It is fundamental to know the behavior of this basic ingredient since the result of the dough will be very different according to the grinding and the cereal used. As the flour that is used more frequently is that of wheat, we will focus on it (although without stopping - for now - in its varieties).

In general terms, we could say that wheat flour is composed of starch and other elements (in variable proportions) such as minerals, vitamins, proteins, and ashes. The sifting of the milling influences these factors. The whole grain, keeping the bran, make up the whole flours; if they are deprived of it, we will obtain white flours. There are flours of soft wheat and durum wheat, the difference of these lying in the amount of protein that each contains and, therefore, the result of the bread will be different.

The **proteins (gliadin and glutenin)** that are in the flour are the main things responsible for the formation and elasticity of the dough that, together with the fermentation, makes the bread have volume and consistency. As the flour is hydrated, the proteins bind, transforming into gluten. **When we manipulate a bread dough, and they are oxygenated, the dough becomes elastic and workable.** If the mass is well hydrated and kneaded, a protein mesh (glutinous network) is created that covers it. The more protein the flour has, the more water it will need, so you must be careful not to overdo it.

Yeast is the second great protagonist of bread. Typically, a fungus is used (suitable for ingestion), which can be found in two versions: dry (lyophilized) or fresh. Keep in mind that this latest version is a living organism, so it must be appropriately conserved, as it loses strength over time. If dry is used, the proportion of yeast is 1/3 of the amount indicated in the recipe for fresh. For example, if it calls for 10 gr. of fresh yeast, you should use 3 gr. of dry yeast.

Another way to produce bread is the use of **natural sourdough**, the oldest way to make the bread ferment (through bacteria that are present in the environment). When the bread is made with sourdough, it usually has a slightly acidic taste, lasts longer, has an intense smell, and, due to bacterial fermentation, facilitates digestion. The process of making the sourdough is simple, but it takes time (it usually takes about 5 days). Here you have a good recipe.

Water and salt have no significant complications and secrets. It must be made clear that it is not necessary to use mineral water; tap water works perfectly even if some prefer to filter it. In fact, in the best professional bakeries, no water other than tap water is used. Salt brings flavor, and you can use several types of salts (marine, with herbs, etc.). In fact, the bread doesn't have to have salt; many loaves are traditionally bland, and others are brushed with a saline solution when leaving the oven (especially the loaves with little crumbs).

Flour, yeast, water, and salt are all the essential ingredients you need to make a good bread dough. Before carrying it to the oven comes the work of fermentation, kneading, etc. But as a useful note (and to encourage you to make bread), we must remember that not all the loaves are baked, nor do they need many hours of fermentation and kneading.

There is the bread that can be made in a pan, griddle, casserole, or steamed, and are an excellent option for when you do not want to heat the oven. You can also make many other pieces of bread in skillets, such as pita bread, Moroccan bread, bread from North Africa, and a variety of flatbreads. Making bread in a pan is one of the eldest ways of cooking it. If you decide to make bread in the pan, you must choose a good one that keeps the heat well and can cook evenly.

EVERYDAY PLEASURE

CRISP WHITE BREAD

Makes: 1 pound loaf / 10 slices | Cooking Time: 3 4 hours

Crust Type: Medium | Program: Basic/White Bread

¾ cup lukewarm water (80°F)

1 tablespoon butter, melted

1 tablespoon white sugar

¾ teaspoon sea salt

2 tablespoons milk powder

2 cups wheat flour

¾ teaspoon active dry yeast

PROCESS:

1. Prepare all of the ingredients for your bread and measuring means (a cup, a spoon, kitchen scales).

2. Carefully measure the ingredients into the pan.

3. Place all of the ingredients into the bread bucket in the right order, following the manual for your bread machine.

4. Close the cover.

5. Select the program of your bread machine to BASIC / WHITE BREAD and choose the crust color to MEDIUM.

6. Press START.

7. Wait until the program completes.

8. When done, take the bucket out and let it cool for 5-10 minutes.

9. Shake the loaf from the pan and let cool for 30 minutes on a cooling rack.

10. Slice and serve.

NUTRITION FACTS (PER SERVING)

Calories 113; Total Fat 1.4g; Saturated Fat 0.8g; Cholesterol 3g; Sodium 158mg; Total Carbohydrate 21.6g; Dietary Fiber 0.7g; Total Sugars 2.1g; Protein 3.3g, Vitamin D 1mcg, Calcium 24mg, Iron 1mg, Potassium 33mg

MEDITERRANEAN SEMOLINA BREAD

Makes: 1½-pound loaf / 16 slices

Cooking Time: 3½ hours

Crust Type: Medium

Program: Sandwich /Italian Bread

1 cup lukewarm water (80°F)

1 teaspoon salt

2½ tablespoons butter, melted

2½ teaspoons white sugar

2¼ cups all-purpose flour

⅓ cups semolina

1½ teaspoons active dry yeast

1. Prepare all of the ingredients for your bread and measuring means (a cup, a spoon, kitchen scales).

2. Carefully measure the ingredients into the pan.

3. Place all of the ingredients into the bread bucket in the right order, following the manual for your bread machine. Close the cover.

4. Select the program of your bread machine to ITALIAN BREAD / SANDWICH mode and choose the crust color to MEDIUM. Press START.

5. Wait until the program completes.

6. When done, take the bucket out and let it cool for 5-10 minutes.

7. Shake the loaf from the pan and let cool for 30 minutes on a cooling rack.

NUTRITION FACTS (PER SERVING)

Calories 243; Total Fat 8.1g; Saturated Fat 4.9g; Cholesterol 20g; Sodium 203mg; Total Carbohydrate 37g; Dietary Fiber 1.5g; Total Sugars 2.8g; Protein 5.3g, Vitamin D 5mcg, Calcium 10mg, Iron 2mg, Potassium 80mg

MUSTARD SOUR CREAM BREAD

Makes: 2 ½ pounds

Cooking Time: 2 hours

Crust: Medium

Program: Basic/White bread

1¼ cups (320 ml) lukewarm milk

3 tablespoons sunflower oil

3 tablespoons sour cream

2 tablespoons dry mustard

1 egg

½ sachet sugar vanilla

4 cups (690 g) wheat flour

1 teaspoon active dry yeast

2 tablespoons white sugar

2 teaspoons sea salt

1. Prepare all of the ingredients for your bread and measuring means (a cup, a spoon, kitchen scales). Carefully measure the ingredients into the pan.

2. Place all of the ingredients into the bread bucket in the right order, following the manual for your bread machine. Close the cover.

3. Select the program of your bread machine to BASIC and choose the crust color to MEDIUM. Press START.

4. Wait until the program completes.

5. When done, take the bucket out and let it cool for 5-10 minutes.

6. Shake the loaf from the pan and let cool for 30 minutes on a cooling rack.

7. Slice, serve and enjoy the taste of fragrant homemade bread.

NUTRITION FACTS (PER SERVING)

Calories 340; Total Fat 9.2g; Saturated Fat 1.9g; Cholesterol 26g; Sodium 614mg; Total Carbohydrate 54.6g; Dietary Fiber 2.2g; Total Sugars 5.5g; Protein 9.3g

BUTTERMILK BREAD

Makes: 1-pound loaf / 10 slices

Cooking Time: 3 - 4 hours

Crust Type: Medium

Program: Basic/White Bread

⅔ cup lukewarm buttermilk (80°F)

1 tablespoon butter, melted

1 tablespoon white sugar

¾ teaspoon salt

¼ teaspoon baking powder

1¾ cups all-purpose flour

1⅛ teaspoons instant yeast

1. Prepare all of the ingredients for your bread and measuring means (a cup, a spoon, kitchen scales). Carefully measure the ingredients into the pan.

2. Place all of the ingredients into the bread bucket in the right order, following the manual for your bread machine. Close the cover.

3. Select the program of your bread machine to BASIC and choose the crust color to MEDIUM. Press START.

4. Wait until the program completes. When done, take the bucket out and let it cool for 5-10 minutes.

5. Shake the loaf from the pan and let cool for 30 minutes on a cooling rack.

6. Slice, serve and enjoy the taste of fragrant homemade bread.

NUTRITION FACTS (PER SERVING)

Calories 183; Total Fat 2.2g; Saturated Fat 0.9g; Cholesterol 4g; Sodium 223mg; Total Carbohydrate 35.4g; Dietary Fiber 1.3g; Total Sugars 2.1g; Protein 4.8g, Vitamin D 1mcg, Calcium 18mg, Iron 2mg, Potassium 69mg

HONEY RYE BREAD

Makes: 1 ½ pound / 16 slices

Cooking Time: 3 ½ hours

Program: Basic/White bread

Crust: Medium / Dark

2 ¼ cups (350 g) wheat flour

¼ cup (50 g) rye flour

1 cup (200 ml) lukewarm water

1 egg

1 tablespoon olive oil

1 teaspoon salt

1 ½ tablespoon liquid honey

1 teaspoon active dry yeast

1. Prepare all of the ingredients for your bread and measuring means (a cup, a spoon, kitchen scales). Carefully measure the ingredients into the pan.

2. Place all of the ingredients into the bread bucket in the right order, following the manual for your bread machine.

3. Close the cover.

4. Select the program of your bread machine to BASIC and choose the crust color to MEDIUM or DARK. Press START.

5. Wait until the program completes.

6. When done, take the bucket out and let it cool for 5-10 minutes.

7. Shake the loaf from the pan and let cool for 30 minutes on a cooling rack.

8. Slice, serve and enjoy the taste of fragrant homemade bread.

NUTRITION FACTS (PER SERVING)

Calories 177; Total Fat 2.7g; Saturated Fat 0.6g; Cholesterol 20g; Sodium 300mg; Total Carbohydrate 33.1g; Dietary Fiber 2.0g; Total Sugars 3.4g; Protein 5.1g

TOMATO PAPRIKA BREAD

Makes: 1½-pound loaf / 16 slices | Cooking Time: 2 - 3 hours

Crust: Light | Program: Basic/White Bread

1½ teaspoons active dry yeast	1½ tablespoons butter, melted
3 cups bread flour	1 cup lukewarm water
2 tablespoons white sugar	2 teaspoons ground paprika
1 teaspoon salt	1 cup dried tomatoes, chopped

PROCESS:

1. Prepare all of the ingredients for your bread and measuring means (a cup, a spoon, kitchen scales).

2. Carefully measure the ingredients into the pan, except the tomatoes.

3. Place all of the ingredients into the bread bucket in the right order, following the manual for your bread machine. Close the cover.

4. Select the program of your bread machine to BASIC and choose the crust color to MEDIUM or DARK. Press START.

5. After the signal, put the chopped tomatoes to the dough.

6. Wait until the program completes. When done, take the bucket out and let it cool for 5-10 minutes.

7. Shake the loaf from the pan and let cool for 30 minutes on a cooling rack.

8. Slice, serve and enjoy the taste of fragrant homemade bread.

NUTRITION FACTS (PER SERVING)

Calories 133; Total Fat 4.2g; Saturated Fat 2.6g; Cholesterol 10g; Sodium 177mg; Total Carbohydrate 20.5g; Dietary Fiber 1.2g; Total Sugars 1.9g; Protein 3.1g, Vitamin D 3mcg, Calcium 7mg, Iron 1mg, Potassium 87mg

BRAN BREAD

Cooking Time: 3 hours | Makes: 1 pound / 10 slices

Program: Basic/White bread/French bread | Crust: Medium

2 ½ cups (320 g) all-purpose flour, sifted

1 whole egg

¾ cup (40 g) bran

1 cup (240 ml) lukewarm water

1 tablespoon sunflower oil

2 teaspoons brown sugar

1 teaspoon sea salt

1 teaspoon active dry yeast

PROCESS

1. Prepare all of the ingredients for your bread and measuring means (a cup, a spoon, kitchen scales). Carefully measure the ingredients into the pan.

2. Place all of the ingredients into the bread bucket in the right order, following the manual for your bread machine. Close the cover.

3. Select the program of your bread machine to FRENCH BREAD and choose the crust color to MEDIUM. Press START.

4. Wait until the program completes.

5. When done, take the bucket out and let it cool for 5-10 minutes.

6. Shake the loaf from the pan and let cool for 30 minutes on a cooling rack.

7. Slice, serve and enjoy the taste of fragrant homemade bread.

NUTRITION FACTS (PER SERVING)

Calories 307; Total Fat 5.1g; Saturated Fat 0.9g; Cholesterol 33g; Sodium 480mg; Total Carbohydrate 54g; Dietary Fiber 7.9g; Total Sugars 1.8g; Protein 10.2g

HONEY BEER BREAD

Makes: 1½-pound loaf / 14 slices

Cooking Time: 3 hours 20 minutes

Crust: Medium

Program: Basic/White Bread

1⅙ cups light beer, without foam

2 tablespoons liquid honey

1 tablespoon olive oil

1 teaspoon sea salt

1 teaspoon cumin

2¾ cups bread flour

1½ teaspoons active dry yeast

NUTRITION FACTS (PER SERVING)

Calories 210; Total Fat 1.6g; Saturated Fat 0.2g; Cholesterol 0g; Sodium 135mg; Total Carbohydrate 42.3g; Dietary Fiber 1.8g; Total Sugars 2.6g; Protein 5.9g, Vitamin D 0mcg, Calcium 10mg, Iron 3mg, Potassium 91mg

1. Prepare all of the ingredients for your bread and measuring means (a cup, a spoon, kitchen scales).

2. Carefully measure the ingredients into the pan.

3. Place all of the ingredients into the bread bucket in the right order, following the manual for your bread machine.

4. Close the cover.

5. Select the program of your bread machine to BASIC and choose the crust color to MEDIUM.

6. Press START.

7. Wait until the program completes.

8. When done, take the bucket out and let it cool for 5-10 minutes.

9. Shake the loaf from the pan and let cool for 30 minutes on a cooling rack.

10. Slice, serve and enjoy the taste of fragrant homemade bread.

EGG BREAD

Cooking Time: 3 hours

Makes: 1½ pound / 16 slices

Program: Basic | Crust: Medium

4 cups (520 g) bread flour, sifted

1 cup (230 ml) lukewarm milk

2 whole eggs

1 teaspoon active dry yeast

1 ½ teaspoons salt

2 ¼ tablespoons white sugar

1 ½ tablespoons butter, melted

NUTRITION FACTS (PER SERVING)

Calories 319; Total Fat 5.6g; Saturated Fat 2.7g; Cholesterol 56g; Sodium 495mg; Total Carbohydrate 56.7g; Dietary Fiber 1.8g; Total Sugars 6.5g; Protein 9.6g

1. Prepare all of the ingredients for your bread and measuring means (a cup, a spoon, kitchen scales).

2. Carefully measure the ingredients into the pan.

3. Place all of the ingredients into the bread bucket in the right order, following the manual for your bread machine.

4. Close the cover.

5. Select the program of your bread machine to BASIC and choose the crust color to MEDIUM.

6. Press START.

7. Wait until the program completes.

8. When done, take the bucket out and let it cool for 5-10 minutes.

9. Shake the loaf from the pan and let cool for 30 minutes on a cooling rack.

10. Slice, serve and enjoy the taste of fragrant homemade bread.

VEGETABLE VARIETY

CARROT BREAD

Makes: 1 loaf / 8 slices | Cooking Time: 2 hours 10 minutes

Crust: LIGHT | Program: CAKE/SWEET

4 whole eggs

¼ teaspoon sea salt

½ cup (100 g, 4 oz) butter, melted

½ cup (120 g, 4 oz) brown sugar

1 tablespoon vanilla sugar

2 teaspoon ground cinnamon

3 cups (350 g, 13.50 oz) white bread flour

1 tablespoon baking powder

¼ cup (50 g) ground nuts

¾ cup (150 g) carrot, grated

PROCESS

1. Prepare all of the ingredients for your bread and measuring means (a cup, a spoon, kitchen scales).

2. Carefully measure the ingredients into the pan, except the carrots and nuts.

3. Place all of the ingredients into the bread bucket in the right order, following the manual for your bread machine. Close the cover.

4. Select the program of your bread machine to CAKE and choose the crust color to LIGHT. Press START.

5. After the signal, put the grated carrots and nuts to the dough.

6. Wait until the program completes. When done, take the bucket out and let it cool for 5-10 minutes.

7. Shake the loaf from the pan and let cool for 30 minutes on a cooling rack.

8. Cover the prepared bread with icing sugar. Slice, serve and enjoy the taste of fragrant homemade bread.

NUTRITION FACTS (PER SERVING)

Calories 398, Total Fat 17.3 g, Saturated Fat 8.3 g, Cholesterol 112 mg, Sodium 202 mg, Total Carbohydrate 53 g, Dietary Fiber 2.9 g, Total Sugars 14 g, Protein 9.2 g, Vitamin D 16 mcg, Calcium 132 mg, Iron 3 mg, Potassium 381 mg

ZUCCHINI BREAD

Makes: 1 loaf / 8 slices

Cooking Time: 2 hours 10 minutes

Crust: LIGHT | Program: CAKE/SWEET

2 whole eggs

¼ teaspoon sea salt

1 cup (200 ml) olive oil

1 cup (200 g) white sugar

1 tablespoon vanilla sugar

2 teaspoon cinnamon

½ cup (100 g) nuts, ground

3 cups (350 g) bread flour, well sifted

1 tablespoon baking powder

1¼ cup zucchini, grated

1. Prepare all of the ingredients for your bread and measuring means (a cup, a spoon, kitchen scales). Carefully measure the ingredients into the pan, except the zucchini and nuts.

2. Place all of the ingredients into the bread bucket in the right order, following the manual for your bread machine. Close the cover.

3. Select the program of your bread machine to CAKE and choose the crust color to LIGHT. Press START.

4. After the signal, put the grated zucchini and nuts to the dough.

5. Wait until the program completes.

6. When done, take the bucket out and let it cool for 5-10 minutes.

7. Shake the loaf from the pan and let cool for 30 minutes on a cooling rack.

NUTRITION FACTS (PER SERVING)

Calories 556, Total Fat 31g, Saturated Fat 4.3g, Cholesterol 41 mg, Sodium 179 mg, Total Carbohydrate 64.3 g, Dietary Fiber 3.1 g, Total Sugars 26.5 g, Protein 8.6 g, Vitamin D 4 mcg, Calcium 114 mg, Iron 3 mg, Potassium 430 mg

TOMATO ONION BREAD

Cooking Time: 4 hours | Crust: Medium

Makes: 2 pounds / 16 slices

Program: Basic/ Bread with additives

2 cups wheat flour

1 cup wholemeal flour

½ cup lukewarm water (80°F)

4 ¾ ounces (140 ml) lukewarm milk

3 tablespoons virgin olive oil

2 tablespoons white sugar

1 teaspoon salt

2 teaspoons active dry yeast

½ teaspoon baking powder

5 sun-dried tomatoes, chopped

1 onion, finely chopped

¼ teaspoon black pepper, ground

1. Prepare all of the ingredients for your bread and measuring means (a cup, a spoon, kitchen scales). Saute the onion in a frying pan.

2. Carefully measure the ingredients into the pan, except the onion and tomatoes.

3. Place all of the ingredients into the bread bucket in the right order, following the manual for your bread machine. Close the cover.

4. Select the program of your bread machine to BASIC and choose the crust color to MEDIUM. Press START.

5. After the signal, put the onion and tomatoes to the dough. Wait until the program completes.

6. Shake the loaf from the pan and let cool for 30 minutes on a cooling rack.

NUTRITION FACTS (PER SERVING)

Calories 241; Total Fat 6.4g; Saturated Fat 1.1g; Cholesterol 1g; Sodium 305mg; Total Carbohydrate 40g; Dietary Fiber 3.5g; Total Sugars 6.8g; Protein 6.7g

POTATO ROSEMARY BREAD

Makes: 2½ pounds / 20 slices

Cooking Time: 3½ hours

Crust: Medium

Program: Bread with Filling

4 cups bread flour, sifted

1 tablespoon white sugar

1 tablespoon sunflower oil

1½ teaspoons salt

1½ cups lukewarm water

1 teaspoon active dry yeast

1 cup potatoes, mashed

2 teaspoons crushed rosemary

1. Prepare all of the ingredients for your bread and measuring means (a cup, a spoon, kitchen scales). Carefully measure the ingredients into the pan, except the potato and rosemary.

2. Place all of the ingredients into the bread bucket in the right order, following the manual for your bread machine. Close the cover.

3. Select the program of your bread machine to BREAD with FILLINGS and choose the crust color to MEDIUM. Press START.

4. After the signal, put the mashed potato and rosemary to the dough.

5. Wait until the program completes. When done, take the bucket out and let it cool for 5-10 minutes.

6. Shake the loaf from the pan and let cool for 30 minutes on a cooling rack.

NUTRITION FACTS (PER SERVING)

Calories 106; Total Fat 1g; Saturated Fat 0.1g; Cholesterol 0g; Sodium 641mg; Total Carbohydrate 21g; Dietary Fiber 1g; Total Sugars 0.8g; Protein 2.9g, Vitamin D 0mcg, Calcium 7mg, Iron 1mg, Potassium 63mg

SPICY ONION BREAD

Cooking Time: 3 ½ hours

Makes: 2 pounds / 18 slices

Program: Basic | Crust: Medium

1 cup lukewarm water (80°F)

1 tablespoon butter, melted

1 teaspoon sea salt

3 cups wheat flour

3 tablespoons powdered milk

1 tablespoon white sugar

1½ teaspoon onion, lightly toasted

¾ teaspoon black pepper, ground

¼ teaspoon garlic powder

2 teaspoons active dry yeast

1. Prepare all of the ingredients for your bread and measuring means (a cup, a spoon, kitchen scales).

2. Carefully measure the ingredients into the pan, except the spices and onion.

3. Place all of the ingredients into the bread bucket in the right order, following the manual for your bread machine. Close the cover.

4. Select the program of your bread machine to BASIC and choose the crust color to MEDIUM. Press START.

5. After the signal, put the onion and spices to the dough.

6. Wait until the program completes.

7. When done, take the bucket out and let it cool for 5-10 minutes.

8. Shake the loaf from the pan and let cool for 30 minutes on a cooling rack.

NUTRITION FACTS (PER SERVING)
(PER SERVING)

Calories 203; Total Fat 2g; Saturated Fat 1g; Cholesterol 4; Sodium 319mg; Total Carbohydrate 39.6g; Dietary Fiber 1.5g; Total Sugars 3.2g; Protein 6g

CHEESE BROCCOLI CAULIFLOWER BREAD

Makes: 1-pound loaf / 8 slices

Cooking Time: 3 hours 10 minutes

Crust: Medium

Program: Basic/White Bread

¼ cup lukewarm water (80°F)

4 tablespoons extra virgin olive oil

1 egg white

1 teaspoon fresh lemon juice

2/3 cup cheddar cheese, grated

3 tablespoons green onion

½ cup broccoli, chopped

½ cup cauliflower, chopped

½ teaspoon lemon pepper seasoning

2 cups bread flour

1 teaspoon active dry yeast

1. Prepare all of the ingredients for your bread and measuring means (a cup, a spoon, kitchen scales).

2. Carefully measure the ingredients into the pan, except the vegetables and cheese.

3. Place all of the ingredients into the bread bucket in the right order, following the manual for your bread machine. Close the cover.

4. Select the program of your bread machine to BASIC and choose the crust color to MEDIUM. Press START.

5. After the signal, put the vegetables and cheese to the dough.

6. Wait until the program completes.

7. When done, take the bucket out and let it cool for 5-10 minutes.

8. Shake the loaf from the pan and let cool for 30 minutes on a cooling rack.

NUTRITION FACTS (PER SERVING)

Calories 220; Total Fat 10.5g; Saturated Fat 3.1g; Cholesterol 10g; Sodium 68mg; Total Carbohydrate 25.2g; Dietary Fiber 1.4g; Total Sugars 0.5g; Protein 6.6g, Vitamin D 1mcg, Calcium 80mg, Iron 2mg, Potassium 105mg

SPINACH BREAD

Cooking: 3 ½ hours

Makes: 2 pounds / 20 slices

Program: Basic | Crust: Medium

4 cups bread flour, sifted

½ cup frozen spinach

1 cup lukewarm water (80°F)

1 tablespoon olive oil

1½ teaspoon active dry yeast

NUTRITION FACTS (PER SERVING)
(PER SERVING)

Calories 238; Total Fat 1.7g; Saturated Fat 0.2g; Cholesterol 0g; Sodium 3mg; Total Carbohydrate 44.4g; Dietary Fiber 0.2g; Total Sugars 2g; Protein 8.3g

1. Defrost the spinach.

2. Prepare all of the ingredients for your bread and measuring means (a cup, a spoon, kitchen scales).

3. Carefully measure the ingredients into the pan, except the spinach.

4. Place all of the ingredients into the bread bucket in the right order, following the manual for your bread machine. Close the cover.

5. Select the program of your bread machine to BASIC and choose the crust color to MEDIUM. Press START.

6. After the signal, put the spinach to the dough.

7. Wait until the program completes.

8. When done, take the bucket out and let it cool for 5-10 minutes.

9. Shake the loaf from the pan and let cool for 30 minutes on a cooling rack.

10. Slice, serve and enjoy the taste of fragrant homemade bread.

BEETROOT PRUNE BREAD

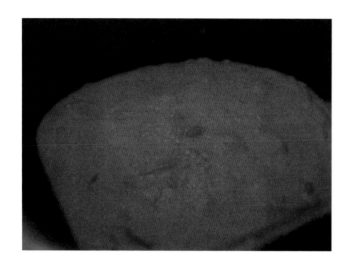

Cooking Time: 3½ hours

Makes: 2½ pounds / 20 slices

Program: Basic | Crust: Medium

1½ cups lukewarm beet broth

5¼ cups all-purpose flour

1 cup beet puree

1 cup prunes, chopped

4 tablespoons extra virgin olive oil

2 tablespoons dry cream

1 tablespoon brown sugar

2 teaspoons active dry yeast

1 tablespoon whole milk

2 teaspoons sea salt

1. Prepare all of the ingredients for your bread and measuring means (a cup, a spoon, kitchen scales).

2. Carefully measure the ingredients into the pan, except the prunes.

3. Place all of the ingredients into the bread bucket in the right order, following the manual for your bread machine. Close the cover.

4. Select the program of your bread machine to BASIC and choose the crust color to MEDIUM. Press START.

5. After the signal, put the prunes to the dough. Wait until the program completes.

6. When done, take the bucket out and let it cool for 5-10 minutes.

7. Shake the loaf from the pan and let cool for 30 minutes on a cooling rack.

8. Slice, serve and enjoy the taste of fragrant homemade bread.

NUTRITION FACTS (PER SERVING)

Calories 443; Total Fat 8.2g; Saturated Fat 1.3g; Cholesterol 1g; Sodium 604mg; Total Carbohydrate 81.1g; Dietary Fiber 4.4g; Total Sugars 11.7g; Protein 9.9g

HERB BREAD

Makes: 1-pound loaf / 8 slices

Cooking Time: 3 hours 10 minutes

Crust: Medium

Program: Basic/White Bread

½ cup green onion, sliced

½ teaspoon dried basil

½ teaspoon dried thyme

¼ teaspoon dried rosemary

2 tablespoons butter, melted

1 cup whole milk

1 whole egg

2 tablespoons white sugar

¾ teaspoons salt

3 cups all-purpose flour

2 teaspoons active dry yeast

1. Prepare all of the ingredients for your bread and measuring means (a cup, a spoon, kitchen scales).

2. Carefully measure the ingredients into the pan.

3. Place all of the ingredients into the bread bucket in the right order, following the manual for your bread machine. Close the cover.

4. Select the program of your bread machine to BASIC and choose the crust color to MEDIUM. Press START.

5. Wait until the program completes.

6. When done, take the bucket out and let it cool for 5-10 minutes.

7. Shake the loaf from the pan and let cool for 30 minutes on a cooling rack.

8. Slice, serve and enjoy the taste of fragrant homemade bread.

NUTRITION FACTS (PER SERVING)

Calories 239; Total Fat 5g; Saturated Fat 2.6g; Cholesterol 31g; Sodium 260mg; Total Carbohydrate 41.2g; Dietary Fiber 1.7g; Total Sugars 4.9g; Protein 7g, Vitamin D 16mcg, Calcium 52mg, Iron 3mg, Potassium 140mg

MUSHROOM BREAD

Cooking Time: 3½ hours

Makes: 2 pounds / 20 slices

Program: Basic | Crust: Medium

4 cups all-purpose flour

½ cup lukewarm water (80°F)

1 cup your favorite mushrooms, dried

1 tablespoon melted butter

2 teaspoons white sugar

2 egg yolks, lightly beaten

1 teaspoon active dry yeast

1 teaspoon sea salt

NUTRITION FACTS (PER SERVING)

Calories 261; Total Fat 3.2g; Saturated Fat 1.4g; Cholesterol 56g; Sodium 305mg; Total Carbohydrate 49.3g; Dietary Fiber 1.9g; Total Sugars 1.3g; Protein 7.6g

1. Put the mushrooms to the 200 ml of boiling water. Leave for 1 hour, drain (and keep) the broth.

2. Finely chop the mushrooms.

3. Prepare all of the ingredients for your bread and measuring means (a cup, a spoon, kitchen scales). Carefully measure the ingredients into the pan.

4. Place all of the ingredients, including the mushroom broth, into the bread bucket in the right order, following the manual for your bread machine. Close the cover.

5. Select the program of your bread machine to BASIC and choose the crust color to MEDIUM. Press START.

6. Wait until the program completes.

7. When done, take the bucket out and let it cool for 5-10 minutes.

8. Shake the loaf from the pan and let cool for 30 minutes on a cooling rack.

9. Slice, serve and enjoy the taste of fragrant homemade bread.

SAVORY LOAVES

LAVENDER BREAD

Makes: 1-pound loaf / 8 slices

Cooking Time: 2 - 3 hours

Crust: Medium

Program: Basic/White Bread

¾ cup lukewarm milk (80°F)

1 tablespoon butter, melted

1 tablespoon brown sugar

¾ teaspoon salt

1 teaspoon fresh lavender flower

¼ teaspoon lemon zest

¼ teaspoon fresh thyme, chopped

2 cups all-purpose flour, sifted

¾ teaspoon active dry yeast

1. Prepare all of the ingredients for your bread and measuring means (a cup, a spoon, kitchen scales).

2. Carefully measure the ingredients into the pan. Place all of the ingredients, into the bread bucket in the right order, following the manual for your bread machine. Close the cover.

3. Select the program of your bread machine to BASIC and choose the crust color to MEDIUM. Press START.

4. Wait until the program completes.

5. When done, take the bucket out and let it cool for 5-10 minutes.

6. Shake the loaf from the pan and let cool for 30 minutes on a cooling rack.

NUTRITION FACTS (PER SERVING)

Calories 133; Total Fat 1.8g; Saturated Fat 1g; Cholesterol 4g; Sodium 228mg; Total Carbohydrate 25.3g; Dietary Fiber 0.9g; Total Sugars 1.2g; Protein 3.4g, Vitamin D 1mcg, Calcium 10mg, Iron 2mg, Potassium 43mg

MUSTARD BEER BREAD

Cooking Time: 3 ½ hours

Makes: 2 pounds / 20 slices

Program: Basic

Crust: Medium

INGREDIENTS

4 cups (500 g) all-purpose flour

10 ounces (300 ml) dark beer

3 tablespoons granular mustard

1 teaspoon Dijon mustard

1 tablespoon butter, melted

1 tablespoon black molasses

1 teaspoon active dry yeast

1 teaspoon sea salt

PROCESS

1. Prepare all of the ingredients for your bread and measuring means (a cup, a spoon, kitchen scales).

2. Carefully measure the ingredients into the pan.

3. Place all of the ingredients, into the bread bucket in the right order, following the manual for your bread machine.

4. Close the cover.

5. Select the program of your bread machine to BASIC and choose the crust color to MEDIUM.

6. Press START.

7. Wait until the program completes.

8. When done, take the bucket out and let it cool for 5-10 minutes.

9. Shake the loaf from the pan and let cool for 30 minutes on a cooling rack.

10. Slice, serve and enjoy the taste of fragrant homemade bread.

NUTRITION FACTS (PER SERVING)

Calories 284

Total Fat 3.3g

Saturated Fat 1.1g

Cholesterol 4g

Sodium 305mg

Total Carbohydrate 52.5g

Dietary Fiber 2.4g

Total Sugars 1.9g

Protein 7.9g

MEDITERRANEAN OLIVE BREAD

Cooking Time: 3½ hours

Makes: 2½ pounds / 24 slices

Program: Basic | Crust: Medium

INGREDIENTS

4 cups bread flour

1 cup black/green olives, sliced

1 teaspoon active dry yeast

3 tablespoons extra virgin olive oil

1 tablespoon white sugar

1 ½ cups lukewarm water (80°F)

1 ½ teaspoons sea salt

PROCESS

1. Prepare all of the ingredients for your bread and measuring means (a cup, a spoon, kitchen scales).

2. Carefully measure the ingredients into the pan.

3. Place all of the ingredients, into the bread bucket in the right order, following the manual for your bread machine.

4. Close the cover.

5. Select the program of your bread machine to BASIC and choose the crust color to MEDIUM.

6. Press START.

7. Wait until the program completes.

8. When done, take the bucket out and let it cool for 5-10 minutes.

9. Shake the loaf from the pan and let cool for 30 minutes on a cooling rack.

10. Slice, serve with some olives and enjoy the taste of fragrant homemade bread.

NUTRITION FACTS (PER SERVING) (PER SERVING)

Calories 299; Total Fat 7.7g; Saturated Fat 1.1g; Cholesterol 0g; Sodium 587mg; Total Carbohydrate 50.4g; Dietary Fiber 2.3g; Total Sugars 1.7g; Protein 6.8g

BLUE CHEESE ONION BREAD

Makes: 1-pound loaf / 10 slices

Cooking Time: 3 hours 10 minutes

Crust: Light

Program: Basic/White Bread

¾ cup lukewarm water (80°F)

1 whole egg

2 teaspoons butter, melted

3 tablespoons powdered skim milk

2 teaspoons white sugar

½ teaspoon kosher salt

1/3 cup blue cheese, crumbled

2 teaspoons dried onion flakes

2 cups all-purpose flour, sifted

3 tablespoons potato flakes, mashed

¾ teaspoons active dry yeast

1. Prepare all of the ingredients for your bread and measuring means (a cup, a spoon, kitchen scales).

2. Carefully measure the ingredients into the pan.

3. Place all of the ingredients, into the bread bucket in the right order, following the manual for your bread machine. Close the cover.

4. Select the program of your bread machine to BASIC and choose the crust color to MEDIUM. Press START.

5. Wait until the program completes.

6. When done, take the bucket out and let it cool for 5-10 minutes.

7. Shake the loaf from the pan and let cool for 30 minutes on a cooling rack.

8. Slice, serve with some olives and enjoy the taste of fragrant homemade bread.

NUTRITION FACTS (PER SERVING)

Calories 134; Total Fat 2.8g; Saturated Fat 1.5g; Cholesterol 22g; Sodium 201mg; Total Carbohydrate 21.9g; Dietary Fiber 0.8g; Total Sugars 1.9g; Protein 4.9g, Vitamin D 16mcg, Calcium 46mg, Iron 1mg, Potassium 91mg

ONION BACON BREAD

Cooking Time: 3 hours

Makes: 2½ pounds / 22 slices

Program: Basic | Crust: Medium

1 ½ cups lukewarm water (80°F)

2 tablespoons sugar

3 teaspoons active dry yeast

4 ½ cups wheat flour

1 whole egg

2 teaspoons kosher salt

1 tablespoon olive oil

3 small onions, chopped and lightly toasted

1 cup bacon, chopped

1. Prepare all of the ingredients for your bread and measuring means (a cup, a spoon, kitchen scales).

2. Carefully measure the ingredients into the pan, except the bacon and onion.

3. Place all of the ingredients, into the bread bucket in the right order, following the manual for your bread machine. Close the cover.

4. Select the program of your bread machine to BASIC and choose the crust color to MEDIUM. Press START.

5. After the machine beeps, add the onion and bacon.

6. Wait until the program completes.

7. When done, take the bucket out and let it cool for 5-10 minutes.

8. Shake the loaf from the pan and let cool for 30 minutes on a cooling rack.

NUTRITION FACTS (PER SERVING)

Calories 391; Total Fat 9.7g; Saturated Fat 2.7g; Cholesterol 38g; Sodium 960mg; Total Carbohydrate 59.9g; Dietary Fiber 2.8g; Total Sugars 4.3g; Protein 14.7g

GARLIC CREAM CHEESE BREAD

Makes: 1 pound /8 slices

Cooking Time: 2 - 3 hours

Crust: Medium

Program: Basic/White Bread

⅓ cup lukewarm water (80°F)

⅓ cup herb garlic cream cheese mix, at room temperature

1 whole egg, beaten, at room temp

4 teaspoons butter, melted

1 tablespoon white sugar

⅔ teaspoon sea salt

2 cups all-purpose flour

1 teaspoon active dry yeast

1. Prepare all of the ingredients for your bread and measuring means (a cup, a spoon, kitchen scales).

2. Carefully measure the ingredients into the pan.

3. Place all of the ingredients, into the bread bucket in the right order, following the manual for your bread machine. Close the cover.

4. Select the program of your bread machine to BASIC and choose the crust color to MEDIUM. Press START.

5. Wait until the program completes.

6. When done, take the bucket out and let it cool for 5-10 minutes.

7. Shake the loaf from the pan and let cool for 30 minutes on a cooling rack.

8. Slice, serve and enjoy the taste of fragrant homemade bread.

NUTRITION FACTS (PER SERVING)

Calories 179; Total Fat 6.2g; Saturated Fat 3.5g; Cholesterol 36g; Sodium 207mg; Total Carbohydrate 25.9g; Dietary Fiber 1g; Total Sugars 1.6g; Protein 4.9g, Vitamin D 3mcg, Calcium 16mg, Iron 2mg, Potassium 63mg

FISH BELL PEPPER BRAN BREAD

2 ½ cups wheat flour

½ cup bran

11/3 cups lukewarm water

1½ teaspoons salt

1½ teaspoons brown sugar

1½ tablespoon mustard oil

1¼ teaspoon active dry yeast

2 teaspoons powdered milk

1 cup bell pepper, chopped

¾ cup smoked fish, chopped

1 onion, chopped and lightly fried

Cooking Time: 3 hours

Makes: 2 pounds / 20 slices

Program: Basic | Crust: Medium

NUTRITION FACTS (PER SERVING)

Calories 208; Total Fat 3.8g; Saturated Fat 0.5g; Cholesterol 8g; Sodium 487mg; Total Carbohydrate 35.9g; Dietary Fiber 4.2g; Total Sugars 2.7g; Protein 7.2g

1. Prepare all of the ingredients for your bread and measuring means (a cup, a spoon, kitchen scales).

2. Carefully measure the ingredients into the pan, except the vegetables and fish.

3. Place all of the ingredients, into the bread bucket in the right order, following the manual for your bread machine. Close the cover.

4. Select the program of your bread machine to BASIC and choose the crust color to MEDIUM. Press START.

5. After the signal, add all the additives. Wait until the program completes.

6. When done, take the bucket out and let it cool for 5-10 minutes.

7. Shake the loaf from the pan and let cool for 30 minutes on a cooling rack.

ROSEMARY BREAD

Makes: 1-pound loaf / 8 slices

Cooking Time: 2 - 3 hours

Crust: Medium | Program: Basic/White Bread

INGREDIENTS:

¾ cup lukewarm water (80°F)

1⅔ tablespoons melted butter, cooled

2 teaspoons white sugar

1 teaspoon kosher salt

1 tablespoon fresh rosemary, chopped

2 cups bread flour

1⅓ teaspoons instant yeast

PROCESS:

1. Prepare all of the ingredients for your bread and measuring means (a cup, a spoon, kitchen scales).

2. Carefully measure the ingredients into the pan, except the rosemary.

3. Place all of the ingredients, into the bread bucket in the right order, following the manual for your bread machine.

4. Close the cover.

5. Select the program of your bread machine to BASIC and choose the crust color to MEDIUM.

6. Press START.

7. After the signal, add the rosemary.

8. Wait until the program completes.

9. When done, take the bucket out and let it cool for 5-10 minutes.

10. Shake the loaf from the pan and let cool for 30 minutes on a cooling rack.

11. Slice, serve and enjoy the taste of fragrant homemade bread.

NUTRITION FACTS (PER SERVING)

Calories 175

Total Fat 6.2g

Saturated Fat 3.7g

Cholesterol 15g

Sodium 333mg

Total Carbohydrate 25.8g

Dietary Fiber 1.4g

Total Sugars 1.1g

Protein 4g

Vitamin D 4mcg

Calcium 13mg

Iron 2mg

Potassium 76mg

LAVENDER BREAD

INGREDIENTS

1 ½ cups white wheat flour, sifted

2 1/3 cups wholemeal flour

1 teaspoon fresh yeast

1 ½ cups lukewarm water

1 teaspoon lavender

1 ½ tablespoon honey, liquid

1 teaspoon salt

PROCESS

1. Prepare all of the ingredients for your bread and measuring means (a cup, a spoon, kitchen scales).

2. Carefully measure the ingredients into the pan, except the lavender.

3. Place all of the ingredients, into the bread bucket in the right order, following the manual for your bread machine. Close the cover.

4. Select the program of your bread machine to BASIC and choose the crust color to MEDIUM.

5. Press START. After the signal, add the lavender. Wait until the program completes.

6. When done, take the bucket out and let it cool for 5-10 minutes.

7. Shake the loaf from the pan and let cool for 30 minutes on a cooling rack.

8. Slice, serve and enjoy the taste of fragrant homemade bread.

NUTRITION FACTS (PER SERVING)

Calories 226; Total Fat 1.1g; Saturated Fat 0g; Cholesterol 0g; Sodium 293mg; Total Carbohydrate 46.1g; Dietary Fiber 4.4g; Total Sugars 3.3g; Protein 7.5g

SALAMI BREAD

Makes: 1-pound loaf / 8 slices

Cooking Time: 3 hours 10 minutes

Crust: Light

Program: Basic/White Bread

¾ cup lukewarm water (80°F)

1/3 cup shredded mozzarella cheese

4 teaspoons sugar

2/3 teaspoon salt

2/3 teaspoon dried basil

1/3 teaspoon garlic powder

2 cups + 2 tablespoons wheat flour

1 teaspoon active dry yeast

½ cup finely diced hot salami

1. Prepare all of the ingredients for your bread and measuring means (a cup, a spoon, kitchen scales).

2. Carefully measure the ingredients into the pan, except the salami.

3. Place all of the ingredients, into the bread bucket in the right order, following the manual for your bread machine. Close the cover.

4. Select the program of your bread machine to BASIC and choose the crust color to LIGHT. Press START.

5. After the signal, add the salami.

6. Wait until the program completes.

7. When done, take the bucket out and let it cool for 5-10 minutes.

8. Shake the loaf from the pan and let cool for 30 minutes on a cooling rack.

9. Slice, serve and enjoy the taste of fragrant homemade bread.

NUTRITION FACTS (PER SERVING)

Calories 163; Total Fat 2.5g; Saturated Fat 1g; Cholesterol 6g; Sodium 290mg; Total Carbohydrate 28.6g; Dietary Fiber 1g; Total Sugars 2.3g; Protein 5.8g, Vitamin D 4mcg, Calcium 7mg, Iron 2mg, Potassium 62mg

PERFECT FOR DINNER

CORN SOUR CREAM BREAD

Makes: 2-pound / 16 slices | Cooking Time: 3½ hours

Crust: Medium | Program: Basic/White Bread

3½ cups all-purpose flour	2 teaspoons active dry yeast
1¾ cups cornflour	2 teaspoons salt
5 ounces sour cream	16 ¼ ounces lukewarm water
2 tablespoons corn oil	poppy seeds for sprinkling

PROCESS:

1. Prepare all of the ingredients for your bread and measuring means (a cup, a spoon, kitchen scales).

2. Carefully measure the ingredients into the pan.

3. Place all of the ingredients, into the bread bucket in the right order, following the manual for your bread machine. Close the cover.

4. Select the program of your bread machine to BASIC and choose the crust color to MEDIUM.

5. Press START.

6. After the kneading, brush the loaf with the water and sprinkle with poppy seeds.

7. Wait until the program completes.

8. When done, take the bucket out and let it cool for 5-10 minutes.

9. Shake the loaf from the pan and let cool for 30 minutes on a cooling rack.

10. Slice, serve and enjoy the taste of fragrant homemade bread.

NUTRITION FACTS (PER SERVING)

Calories 223; Total Fat 4.8g; Saturated Fat 1.6g; Cholesterol 4g; Sodium 297mg; Total Carbohydrate 39.9g; Dietary Fiber 2.6g; Total Sugars 0.2g; Protein 5.2g, Vitamin D 0mcg, Calcium 16mg, Iron 2mg, Potassium 117mg

OATMEAL BREAD

Cooking Time: 3 hours | Makes: 1½ pound / 12 slices

Program: Basic/White Bread | Crust: Medium

1½ teaspoon active dry yeast

2 cups (350 g) white bread flour, sifted

½ cup (100 g) oatmeal flour

1 teaspoon salt

2 tablespoons liquid honey (can be replaced with sugar)

½ cup (150 ml) yogurt

1 tablespoon butter, melted

¾ cup (200 ml) lukewarm water (80°F)

2 tablespoons oatmeal flakes

PROCESS

1. Prepare all of the ingredients for your bread and measuring means (a cup, a spoon, kitchen scales).

2. Carefully measure the ingredients into the pan.

3. Place all of the ingredients, into the bread bucket in the right order, following the manual for your bread machine.

4. Close the cover.

5. Select the program of your bread machine to BASIC and choose the crust color to MEDIUM.

6. Press START.

7. After the kneading, lubricate the surface of the loaf with water or egg yolk and sprinkle with oat flakes.

8. Wait until the program completes.

9. When done, take the bucket out and let it cool for 5-10 minutes.

10. Shake the loaf from the pan and let cool for 30 minutes on a cooling rack.

11. Slice, serve and enjoy the taste of fragrant homemade bread.

NUTRITION FACTS (PER SERVING)

Calories 176; Total Fat 2.3g; Saturated Fat 1.2g; Sodium 313mg; Total Carbohydrate 32.9g; Dietary Fiber 1.6g; Total Sugars 5.5g; Protein 5.5g

SIMPLE DARK RYE BREAD

Makes: 1-pound loaf / 8 slices

Cooking Time: 2 - 3 hours

Crust: Medium

Program: Basic/White Bread

⅔ cup lukewarm water (80°F)

1 tablespoon melted butter, cooled

¼ cup molasses

¼ teaspoon salt

1 tablespoon unsweetened cocoa powder

½ cup rye flour

pinch of ground nutmeg

1¼ cups white wheat flour, sifted

1⅛ teaspoons active dry yeast

1. Prepare all of the ingredients for your bread and measuring means (a cup, a spoon, kitchen scales).

2. Carefully measure the ingredients into the pan.

3. Place all of the ingredients, into the bread bucket in the right order, following the manual for your bread machine. Close the cover.

4. Select the program of your bread machine to BASIC and choose the crust color to MEDIUM. Press START.

5. Wait until the program completes.

6. When done, take the bucket out and let it cool for 5-10 minutes.

7. Shake the loaf from the pan and let cool for 30 minutes on a cooling rack.

8. Slice, serve and enjoy the taste of fragrant homemade bread.

NUTRITION FACTS (PER SERVING)

Calories 151; Total Fat 2.1g; Saturated Fat 1g; Cholesterol 4g; Sodium 88mg; Total Carbohydrate 29.4g; Dietary Fiber 2.7g; Total Sugars 5.9g; Protein 4.2g, Vitamin D 1mcg, Calcium 30mg, Iron 2mg, Potassium 241mg

WALNUT BREAD

Cooking Time: 4 hours

Makes: 2 pounds / 20 slices

Program: French bread

Crust: Medium

4 cups (500 g) wheat flour, sifted

½ cup (130 ml) lukewarm water (80°F)

½ cup (120 ml) lukewarm milk (80°F)

2 whole eggs

½ cup walnuts, fried and chopped

1 tablespoon walnut oil

1 tablespoon brown sugar

1 teaspoon salt

1 teaspoon active dry yeast

1. Prepare all of the ingredients for your bread and measuring means (a cup, a spoon, kitchen scales).

2. Carefully measure the ingredients into the pan.

3. Place all of the ingredients, into the bread bucket in the right order, following the manual for your bread machine. Close the cover.

4. Select the program of your bread machine to FRENCH BREAD and choose the crust color to MEDIUM.

5. Press START. Wait until the program completes.

6. When done, take the bucket out and let it cool for 5-10 minutes.

7. Shake the loaf from the pan and let cool for 30 minutes on a cooling rack.

8. Slice, serve and enjoy the taste of fragrant homemade bread.

NUTRITION FACTS (PER SERVING)

Calories 257; Total Fat 6.7g; Saturated Fat 1g; Cholesterol 34g; Sodium 252mg; Total Carbohydrate 40.8g; Dietary Fiber 1.9g; Total Sugars 2g; Protein 8.3g

MULTIGRAIN BREAD

Makes: 1-pound loaf / 8 slices

Cooking Time: 2 - 3 hours

Crust: Medium

Program: Basic/White Bread

¾ cup lukewarm water (80°F)

1 tablespoon melted butter

½ tablespoon liquid honey

½ teaspoon salt

¾ cup multigrain flour

1⅓ cups wheat flour

1 teaspoon active dry yeast

1. Prepare all of the ingredients for your bread and measuring means (a cup, a spoon, kitchen scales).

2. Carefully measure the ingredients into the pan.

3. Place all of the ingredients, into the bread bucket in the right order, following the manual for your bread machine. Close the cover.

4. Select the program of your bread machine to FRENCH BREAD and choose the crust color to MEDIUM.

5. Press START. Wait until the program completes.

6. When done, take the bucket out and let it cool for 5-10 minutes.

7. Shake the loaf from the pan and let cool for 30 minutes on a cooling rack.

8. Slice, serve and enjoy the taste of fragrant homemade bread.

NUTRITION FACTS (PER SERVING)

Calories 124; Total Fat 2.8g; Saturated Fat 1.1g; Cholesterol 4g; Sodium 207mg; Total Carbohydrate 22.8g; Dietary Fiber 3.3g; Total Sugars 1.5g; Protein 4.6g, Vitamin D 1mcg, Calcium 12mg, Iron 1mg, Potassium 33mg

SAUERKRAUT BREAD

Cooking Time: 3 ½ hours

Makes: 2½ pounds / 22 slices

Program: Basic | Crust: Dark

1 cup lukewarm water (80°F)

¼ cup cabbage brine

½ cup finely chopped cabbage

2 tablespoons sunflower oil

2 teaspoons white sugar

1 ½ teaspoons salt

2 1/3 cups rye flour

2 1/3 cups wheat flour

2 teaspoons dry kvass

2 teaspoons active dry yeast

1. Prepare all of the ingredients for your bread and measuring means (a cup, a spoon, kitchen scales).

2. Finely chop the sauerkraut.

3. Carefully measure the ingredients into the pan.

4. Place all of the ingredients, into the bread bucket in the right order, following the manual for your bread machine. Close the cover.

5. Select the program of your bread machine to BASIC and choose the crust color to DARK. Press START.

6. Wait until the program completes.

7. When done, take the bucket out and let it cool for 5-10 minutes.

8. Shake the loaf from the pan and let cool for 30 minutes on a cooling rack.

9. Slice, serve and enjoy the taste of fragrant homemade bread.

NUTRITION FACTS (PER SERVING)

Calories 297; Total Fat 4.9g; Saturated Fat 0.5g; Cholesterol 0g; Sodium 442mg; Total Carbohydrate 55.5g; Dietary Fiber 9.7g; Total Sugars 1.6g; Protein 9.5g

RICE BREAD

Makes: 2-pound / 16 slices

Cooking Time: 3½ hours

Crust: Medium

Program: Basic/White Bread

4½ cups all-purpose flour

1 cup rice, cooked

1 whole egg, beaten

2 tablespoons milk powder

2 teaspoons active dry yeast

2 tablespoons butter, melted

1 tablespoon sugar

2 teaspoon salt

1 ¼ cups lukewarm water (80°F)

1. Prepare all of the ingredients for your bread and measuring means (a cup, a spoon, kitchen scales).

2. Carefully measure the ingredients into the pan.

3. Place all of the ingredients, into the bread bucket in the right order, following the manual for your bread machine. Close the cover.

4. Select the program of your bread machine to BASIC and choose the crust color to MEDIUM. Press START.

5. Wait until the program completes.

6. When done, take the bucket out and let it cool for 5-10 minutes.

7. Shake the loaf from the pan and let cool for 30 minutes on a cooling rack.

8. Slice, serve and enjoy the taste of fragrant homemade bread.

NUTRITION FACTS (PER SERVING)

Calories 197; Total Fat 2.1g; Saturated Fat 1.1g; Cholesterol 14g; Sodium 311mg; Total Carbohydrate 37.8g; Dietary Fiber 1.3g; Total Sugars 1.4g; Protein 5.6g, Vitamin D 2mcg, Calcium 23mg, Iron 2mg, Potassium 55mg

RICE WHEAT BREAD

Cooking Time: 3½ hours

Makes: 2½ pounds / 22 slices

Program: Basic | Crust: Medium

4 ½ cups (580 g) wheat bread flour

1 cup (200 g) rice, cooked

1 whole egg

2 tablespoons soy sauce

2 teaspoons active dried yeast

2 tablespoons melted butter

1 tablespoon brown sugar

2 teaspoons kosher salt

1. Prepare all of the ingredients for your bread and measuring means (a cup, a spoon, kitchen scales).

2. Carefully measure the ingredients into the pan.

3. Place all of the ingredients, into the bread bucket in the right order, following the manual for your bread machine. Close the cover.

4. Select the program of your bread machine to BASIC and choose the crust color to MEDIUM. Press START.

5. Wait until the program completes.

6. When done, take the bucket out and let it cool for 5-10 minutes.

7. Shake the loaf from the pan and let cool for 30 minutes on a cooling rack.

8. Slice, serve and enjoy the taste of fragrant homemade bread.

NUTRITION FACTS (PER SERVING)

Calories 321; Total Fat 4.2g; Saturated Fat 2.1g; Cholesterol 28g; Sodium 837mg; Total Carbohydrate 60.4g; Dietary Fiber 2.2g; Total Sugars 1.4g; Protein 9.1g

PEPPER BREAD

Makes: 1 pound / 8 slices

Cooking Time: 3 hours 10 minutes

Crust: Medium

Program: Basic/White Bread

¾ cup + 1 tablespoon lukewarm milk

3 tablespoons ground red pepper

4 teaspoons fresh red pepper, chopped and roasted

2 tablespoons butter, melted

2 tablespoons brown sugar

2/3 teaspoon salt

2 cups wheat flour

1 teaspoon active dry yeast

1. Prepare all of the ingredients for your bread and measuring means (a cup, a spoon, kitchen scales).

2. Carefully measure the ingredients into the pan.

3. Place all of the ingredients, into the bread bucket in the right order, following the manual for your bread machine. Close the cover.

4. Select the program of your bread machine to BASIC and choose the crust color to MEDIUM. Press START.

5. Wait until the program completes.

6. When done, take the bucket out and let it cool for 5-10 minutes.

7. Shake the loaf from the pan and let cool for 30 minutes on a cooling rack.

8. Slice, serve and enjoy the taste of fragrant homemade bread.

NUTRITION FACTS (PER SERVING)

Calories 189; Total Fat 4.5g; Saturated Fat 2.4g; Cholesterol 10g; Sodium 34mg; Total Carbohydrate 33g; Dietary Fiber 2.3g; Total Sugars 6.8g; Protein 5.1g, Vitamin D 12mcg, Calcium 43mg, Iron 2mg, Potassium 234mg

GARLIC BREAD

Cooking Time: 3 hours

Makes 2 pounds / 20 slices

Program: Basic | Crust: Medium

1 cup lukewarm milk (80°F)

1/10 cup lukewarm water (80°F)

2¾ cups wheat flour

1 tablespoon liquid honey

1 teaspoon active dry yeast

1 teaspoon salt

2 tablespoons butter, melted

3 tablespoons fresh dill

5 cloves garlic, chopped

1. Prepare all of the ingredients for your bread and measuring means (a cup, a spoon, kitchen scales).

2. Carefully measure the ingredients into the pan.

3. Place all of the ingredients, into the bread bucket in the right order, following the manual for your bread machine. Close the cover.

4. Select the program of your bread machine to BASIC and choose the crust color to MEDIUM. Press START.

5. Wait until the program completes.

6. When done, take the bucket out and let it cool for 5-10 minutes.

7. Shake the loaf from the pan and let cool for 30 minutes on a cooling rack.

8. Slice, serve and enjoy the taste of fragrant homemade bread.

NUTRITION FACTS (PER SERVING)

Calories 212; Total Fat 4g; Saturated Fat 2.3g; Cholesterol 10g; Sodium 330mg; Total Carbohydrate 37.9g; Dietary Fiber 1.5g; Total Sugars 3.7g; Protein 6g

ANISE LEMON BREAD

Makes: 1 pound / 8 slices

Cooking Time: 2 - 3 hours

Crust: Medium | Program: Basic

⅔ cup lukewarm water (80°F)

1 whole egg

2⅔ tablespoons butter, melted and cooled

2⅔ tablespoons liquid honey

⅓ teaspoon salt

⅔ teaspoon anise seeds

⅔ teaspoon lemon zest

2 cups all-purpose flour

1⅓ teaspoons active dry yeast

1. Prepare all of the ingredients for your bread and measuring means (a cup, a spoon, kitchen scales).

2. Carefully measure the ingredients into the pan.

3. Place all of the ingredients, into the bread bucket in the right order, following the manual for your bread machine. Close the cover.

4. Select the program of your bread machine to BASIC and choose the crust color to MEDIUM. Press START.

5. Wait until the program completes.

6. When done, take the bucket out and let it cool for 5-10 minutes.

7. Shake the loaf from the pan and let cool for 30 minutes on a cooling rack.

8. Slice, serve and enjoy the taste of fragrant homemade bread.

NUTRITION FACTS (PER SERVING)

Calories 180; Total Fat 4.8g; Saturated Fat 2.7g; Cholesterol 3.1g; Sodium 133mg; Total Carbohydrate 30g; Dietary Fiber 1g; Total Sugars 5.8g; Protein 4.1g, Vitamin D 5mcg, Calcium 11mg, Iron 2mg, Potassium 62mg

SWEET TEMPTATION

GINGER PRUNE BREAD

Makes: 1 loaf / 8 slices

Cooking Time: 3 hours

Crust: LIGHT | Program: BASIC/SWEET

2 whole eggs

1 cup (250 ml, 8 oz) lukewarm milk

¼ cup (60 g, 2 oz) butter, melted

¼ cup (50 g) brown sugar

4 cups (500 g, 18 oz) bread flour

1 tablespoon active dry yeast

1 teaspoon salt

1 cup (150 g, 8 oz) prunes, chopped

1 tablespoon (10 g) fresh ginger, grated

1. Prepare all of the ingredients for your bread and measuring means (a cup, a spoon, kitchen scales). Carefully measure the ingredients into the pan, except the ginger and prunes.

2. Place all of the ingredients, into the bread bucket in the right order, following the manual for your bread machine. Close the cover.

3. Select the program of your bread machine to BASIC and choose the crust color to MEDIUM. Press START.

4. After the machine beeps, add the ginger and prunes. Wait until the program completes. When done, take the bucket out and let it cool for 5-10 minutes.

NUTRITION FACTS (PER SERVING)

Calories 387, Total Fat 8.3 g, Saturated Fat 4.5 g, Cholesterol 59 mg, Sodium 365 mg, Total Carbohydrate 69 g, Dietary Fiber 3.5 g, Total Sugars 15.1 g, Protein 10.1 g, Vitamin D 8 mcg, Calcium 66 mg, Iron 4 mg, Potassium 286 mg

CHERRY BREAD

Cooking time: 2½ hours | Makes: 1½ pound / 14 slices

Program: Basic | Crust: Medium

INGREDIENTS

½ cup lukewarm water (80°F)

½ cup fruit yogurt

2 ½ tablespoons sugar

2 cups wheat flour, sifted

1½ teaspoon active dry yeast

½ cup dried cherries

PROCESS

1. Prepare all of the ingredients for your bread and measuring means (a cup, a spoon, kitchen scales).

2. Carefully measure the ingredients into the pan, except the cherries.

3. Place all of the ingredients, into the bread bucket in the right order, following the manual for your bread machine.

4. Close the cover.

5. Select the program of your bread machine to BASIC and choose the crust color to MEDIUM.

6. Press START.

7. After the machine beeps, add the cherries.

8. Wait until the program completes.

9. When done, take the bucket out and let it cool for 5-10 minutes.

10. Shake the loaf from the pan and let cool for 30 minutes on a cooling rack.

11. Slice, serve and enjoy the taste of fragrant homemade bread.

NUTRITION FACTS (PER SERVING)

Calories 198

Total Fat 0.8g

Saturated Fat 0.3g

Cholesterol 1

Sodium 13mg

Total Carbohydrate 42.2g

Dietary Fiber 1.6g

Total Sugars 9.4g

Protein 5.5g

PUMPKIN BREAD

Makes: 1-pound loaf / 8 slices

Cooking Time: 2 - 3 hours

Crust: Medium | Program: Quick Bread

butter for grease, melted

1½ cups pumpkin puree

3 whole eggs

1/3 cup butter, melted

1 cup brown sugar

3 cups wheat flour, sifted

1½ teaspoons baking powder

¾ teaspoon ground cinnamon

½ teaspoon baking soda

¼ teaspoon ground nutmeg

¼ teaspoon ground ginger

¼ teaspoon salt

Pinch of ground cloves

1. Prepare all of the ingredients for your bread and measuring means (a cup, a spoon, kitchen scales).

2. Carefully measure the ingredients into the pan.

3. Grease the bucket with butter.

4. Place all of the ingredients, into the bread bucket in the right order, following the manual for your bread machine. Close the cover.

5. Select the program of your bread machine to QUICK BREAD and choose the crust color to MEDIUM. Press START. Wait until the program completes.

6. When done, take the bucket out and let it cool for 5-10 minutes.

7. Shake the loaf from the pan and let cool for 30 minutes on a cooling rack.

NUTRITION FACTS (PER SERVING)

Calories 349; Total Fat 9.8g; Saturated Fat 5.5g; Cholesterol 82g; Sodium 166mg; Total Carbohydrate 58.1g; Dietary Fiber 2.8g; Total Sugars 19.4g; Protein 7.6g, Vitamin D 11mcg, Calcium 88mg, Iron 3mg, Potassium 290mg

EGG LIQUEUR BREAD

Makes: 1 loaf / 8 slices

Cooking Time: 2 hours 10 minutes

Crust: LIGHT

Program: CAKE/SWEET

3 whole eggs

½ cup (100 ml) egg liqueur

½ cup (100 g, 4 oz) butter, melted

½ cup (120 g, 4 oz) brown sugar

1 tablespoon vanilla sugar

2 ½ cups (300 g, 11.25 oz) wheat flour

1 tablespoon baking powder

1. Prepare all of the ingredients for your bread and measuring means (a cup, a spoon, kitchen scales).

2. Carefully measure the ingredients into the pan.

3. Place all of the ingredients, into the bread bucket in the right order, following the manual for your bread machine. Close the cover.

4. Select the program of your bread machine to CAKE and choose the crust color to LIGHT. Press START.

5. Wait until the program completes.

6. When done, take the bucket out and let it cool for 5-10 minutes.

7. Shake the loaf from the pan and let cool for 30 minutes on a cooling rack.

8. Slice, serve and enjoy the taste of fragrant homemade bread.

NUTRITION FACTS (PER SERVING)

Calories 349

Total Fat 14.3 g, Saturated Fat 7.9 g, Cholesterol 92 mg, Sodium 107 mg, Total Carbohydrate 46.8 g, Dietary Fiber 1.1 g, Total Sugars 12.8 g, Protein 6.7 g, Vitamin D 14 mcg, Calcium 99 mg, Iron 2 mg, Potassium 257 mg

BANANA BREAD

Cooking Time: 3 hours

Makes: 1½ pound

Program: Dough/Cake/Baking/Sweet
Bread

Crust: Medium

2 cups wheat flour, sifted

¾ cup brown sugar

2 soft bananas, mashed

3 tablespoons butter, melted

1 teaspoon active dry yeast

2 whole eggs, slightly beaten

½ teaspoon vanilla sugar

½ teaspoon ground cinnamon

15 walnuts, crushed

1. Prepare all of the ingredients for your bread and measuring means (a cup, a spoon, kitchen scales).

2. Carefully measure the ingredients into the pan.

3. Place all of the ingredients, into the bread bucket in the right order, following the manual for your bread machine. Close the cover.

4. Select the program of your bread machine to SWEET BREAD and choose the crust color to MEDIUM. Press START. Wait until the program completes.

5. When done, take the bucket out and let it cool for 5-10 minutes.

6. Shake the loaf from the pan and let cool for 30 minutes on a cooling rack.

7. Slice, serve and enjoy the taste of fragrant homemade bread.

NUTRITION FACTS (PER SERVING)

Calories 373; Total Fat 9.3g; Saturated Fat 4.3g; Cholesterol 70mg; Sodium 63mg; Total Carbohydrate 67.2g; Dietary Fiber 2.8g; Total Sugars 30.1g; Protein 7.3g

RAISIN BREAD

Makes: 1-pound loaf / 8 slices

Cooking Time: 3 hours 10 minutes

Crust: Medium | Program: Basic

1/3 cup lukewarm milk (80°F)

2 whole eggs

4 teaspoons butter, melted and cooled

3 tablespoons sugar

2/3 teaspoons salt

1½ teaspoon lemon zest

2 cups all-purpose flour, sifted

1 1/3 teaspoons active dry yeast

¼ cup slivered almonds

¼ cup seedless raisins

1. Prepare all of the ingredients for your bread and measuring means (a cup, a spoon, kitchen scales).

2. Carefully measure the ingredients into the pan, except the raisins and nuts.

3. Place all of the ingredients, into the bread bucket in the right order, following the manual for your bread machine. Close the cover.

4. Select the program of your bread machine to BASIC and choose the crust color to MEDIUM. Press START.

5. After the signal, add the raisins and nuts to the dough.

6. Wait until the program completes.

7. When done, take the bucket out and let it cool for 5-10 minutes.

8. Shake the loaf from the pan and let cool for 30 minutes on a cooling rack.

NUTRITION FACTS (PER SERVING)

Calories 204; Total Fat 5.2g; Saturated Fat 1.9g; Cholesterol 47g; Sodium 228mg; Total Carbohydrate 33.7g; Dietary Fiber 1.6g; Total Sugars 8.1g; Protein 6.2g, Vitamin D 9mcg, Calcium 34mg, Iron 2mg, Potassium 122mg

LEMON FRUIT BREAD

Makes: 1 loaf / 10 slices

Cooking Time: 3 hours

Crust: LIGHT/MEDIUM

Program: BASIC/SWEET

1 whole egg

1 cup (250 ml, 8 oz) lukewarm milk

¼ cup (60 g, 2 oz) butter, melted

1/3 cup (80 g) white sugar

4 cups (500 g, 18 oz) wheat flour

1 tablespoon active dry yeast

1 teaspoon salt

½ cup (100 g) candied lemons

1½ teaspoon lemon zest, grated

½ cup (50 g) raisins

½ cup (50 g) cashew nuts, chopped

1. Prepare all of the ingredients for your bread and measuring means (a cup, a spoon, kitchen scales).

2. Carefully measure the ingredients into the pan, except the raisins, zest, lemons, and nuts.

3. Place all of the ingredients, into the bread bucket in the right order, following the manual for your bread machine. Close the cover.

4. Select the program of your bread machine to BASIC and choose the crust color to MEDIUM. Press START.

5. After the signal, add the raisins, zest, lemons, and nuts to the dough. Wait until the program completes.

6. When done, take the bucket out and let it cool for 5-10 minutes.

7. Shake the loaf from the pan and let cool for 30 minutes on a cooling rack.

NUTRITION FACTS (PER SERVING):

Calories 438, Total Fat 10.6 g, Saturated Fat 4.9 g, Cholesterol 38 mg, Sodium 358 mg, Total Carbohydrate 76.7 g, Dietary Fiber 2.5 g, Total Sugars 23.1 g, Protein 10 g, Vitamin D 6 mcg, Calcium 60 mg, Iron 4 mg, Potassium 211 mg

LEMON PEANUT BREAD

Cooking Time: 4 hours

Makes: 2 pounds / 20 slices

Program: French | Crust: Light

1 cup lukewarm milk (80°F)

3 cups wheat bread flour

½ cup peanut butter

1½ teaspoon active dry yeast

1 tablespoon powdered milk

1 lemon zest

1 whole egg

1 tablespoon walnut oil

1. Prepare all of the ingredients for your bread and measuring means (a cup, a spoon, kitchen scales).

2. Carefully measure the ingredients into the pan, except the zest.

3. Place all of the ingredients, into the bread bucket in the right order, following the manual for your bread machine. Close the cover.

4. Select the program of your bread machine to FRENCH and choose the crust color to LIGHT. Press START.

5. After the signal, add the zest to the dough. Wait until the program completes.

6. When done, take the bucket out and let it cool for 5-10 minutes.

7. Shake the loaf from the pan and let cool for 30 minutes on a cooling rack.

8. Slice, serve and enjoy the taste of fragrant homemade bread.

NUTRITION FACTS (PER SERVING)

Calories 314; Total Fat 11.5g; Saturated Fat 2.6g; Cholesterol 23mg; Sodium 103mg; Total Carbohydrate 42.5g; Dietary Fiber 2.6g; Total Sugars 4.5g; Protein 11.3g

HAZELNUT HONEY BREAD

Makes: 1-pound loaf / 10 slices

Cooking Time: 3 hours 10 minutes

Crust: Medium

Program: Basic/White Bread

½ cup lukewarm milk (80°F)

2 teaspoons butter, melted and cooled

2 teaspoons liquid honey

2/3 teaspoons salt

1/3 cup cooked wild rice, cooled

1/3 cup whole grain flour

2/3 teaspoons caraway seeds

1 cup wheat flour, sifted

1 teaspoon active dry yeast

1/3 cup hazelnuts, chopped

1. Prepare all of the ingredients for your bread and measuring means (a cup, a spoon, kitchen scales).

2. Carefully measure the ingredients into the pan, except the nuts and seeds.

3. Place all of the ingredients, into the bread bucket in the right order, following the manual for your bread machine. Close the cover.

4. Select the program of your bread machine to BASIC and choose the crust color to MEDIUM. Press START.

5. After the signal, add the nuts and seeds into the dough.

6. Wait until the program completes.

7. When done, take the bucket out and let it cool for 5-10 minutes.

8. Shake the loaf from the pan and let cool for 30 minutes on a cooling rack.

NUTRITION FACTS (PER SERVING)

Calories 113; Total Fat 2.8g; Saturated Fat 0.8g; Cholesterol 3g; Sodium 167mg; Total Carbohydrate 18.7g; Dietary Fiber 1.5g; Total Sugars 2g; Protein 3.6g, Vitamin D 1mcg, Calcium 23mg, Iron 1mg, Potassium 87mg

COCONUT MILK BREAD

Makes: 1 loaf / 10 slices | Cooking Time: 3 hours

Crust: LIGHT/MEDIUM | Program: BASIC/SWEET

INGREDIENTS:

1 whole egg

½ cup (100 ml, 4 oz) lukewarm milk (80°F)

½ cup (120 ml, 4 oz) lukewarm coconut milk (80°F)

¼ cup (50 g, 2 oz) butter, melted and cooled

2 tablespoons (50 g) liquid honey

4 cups (500 g, 18 oz) wheat flour, sifted

1 tablespoon active dry yeast

1 teaspoon salt

½ cup (100 g, 6 oz) coconut chips

PROCESS

1. Prepare all of the ingredients for your bread and measuring means (a cup, a spoon, kitchen scales).

2. Carefully measure the ingredients into the pan, except the coconut chips.

3. Place all of the ingredients, into the bread bucket in the right order, following the manual for your bread machine.

4. Close the cover.

5. Select the program of your bread machine to SWEET and choose the crust color to MEDIUM.

6. Press START.

7. After the signal, add the coconut chips into the dough.

8. Wait until the program completes.

9. When done, take the bucket out and let it cool for 5-10 minutes.

10. Shake the loaf from the pan and let cool for 30 minutes on a cooling rack.

11. Slice, serve and enjoy the taste of fragrant homemade bread.

NUTRITION FACTS (PER SERVING)

Calories 421

Total Fat 15.3 g

Saturated Fat 11.7 g

Cholesterol 37 mg

Sodium 350 mg

Total Carbohydrate 61.9 g

Dietary Fiber 3.2 g

Total Sugars 11.7 g

Protein 9.5 g

Vitamin D 6 mcg

Calcium 33 mg

Iron 4 mg

Potassium 157 mg

KITCHEN TOOLS

PASTRY BRUSH

Basting brush or pastry brush looks similar to a paintbrush. It is made of nylon or plastic fiber. It is used to spread glaze, oil, or butter on food.

BLENDER

It is an essential kitchen appliance used to emulsify, puree, or mix food. It comes with a blender jar designed with a rotating blade made of metal. A motor powers the jar.

KITCHEN SCALE

A kitchen scale is a must-have kitchen tool. Preparing certain types of food without one is practically impossible. Yes, there are cups, but when it comes to dough-based meals, a kitchen scale is necessary equipment. The best example is bread, which is hard to make without a kitchen scale. The reason behind it is because flour is a compressible, and measurement in cups will sometimes just not be accurate. To get your bread dough perfect, we suggest you use kitchen scales. You can find classic and digital ones, but for the best accuracy, choose digital scales. They are so much easier to use, and most of them have very modern and exciting designs.

FROM THE AUTHOR

I've been a **professional chef for over 15 years** and a passionate advocate for healthy food. My areas of expertise include **recipe development, healthy meal plans, and professional cooking.** I help people be healthier and enjoy delicious food.

I love baking since my childhood. I always collect new recipes and develop my own. First, I learned how to bake classic pies, and then plunged into traditional European recipes. I studied the art of baking with the best American and European chefs.

Most of all, I like to experiment with bread. **The bread maker opened incredible opportunities for creativity.** I bake crispbread for soup, meat, sweet bread is for tea, and coffee, thick bread is for toast with jam.

Delicious bread exists for any occasion, and it decorates any table from everyday to festive. My friends always know that they can eat my fresh, fragrant bread with an unexpected filling.

I'm baking at work and at home. In the bakery, my assistants help me, and the technologists and cooks improve the recipes and methods of baking. At home, we bake with my family, even the children participate in this fascinating process.

And I generously share my recipes for the bread machine and the secrets of mastery with my readers. Let your house be filled with the cozy smell of freshly baked bread!

OUR RECOMMENDATIONS

Mediterranean Meal Prep Cookbook: Delicious, Quick and Easy Recipes to Prep, Grab and Go for Busy People. 7-Day Meal Plan

Apple Pie Cookbook: Simple & Delicious Apple Pie Recipes for Home Bakers

If you have a free minute, please leave your review of the book. Your feedback is essential for us, as well as for other readers.

RECIPE INDEX

Copyright